GW01018609

Mr. Lomax's Lichfield

by

Howard Clayton

© Howard Clayton 1991

Published by Howard Clayton, 2A Brownsfield Road, Lichfield, Staffordshire
Printed by J. M. Tatler & Son Ltd., Abbey Street Works, Derby
ISBN 0 9503563 3 6

Introduction

THOMAS GEORGE LOMAX (1783–1873) was the son of a Church of England clergyman who kept a boys' school at Druids Heath, near Aldridge, at the end of the 18th century. Thomas was educated at his father's school, where his interest in books led him to write a history of the Druids of England, inspired, no doubt, by the name of his school. He published it some years later.

In 1809 he set up in business in Lichfield as a bookseller and printer, using premises in Tamworth Street. After only a few months, however, he moved to a new position at the corner of Market Street and Bird Street where, in the tradition of his trade, he described himself as carrying on his business "at the sign of the Johnson's head", and over the door he placed a bust of that great man, Samuel Johnson. The place it occupied can still be traced in the brickwork today.[1]

Mr. Lomax's interest in Johnson was more than just commercial. He became a collector of Johnsoniana and had a wide knowledge of Johnson's works which over the years earned him a reputation nationally in the bookselling trade as an authority on the subject.

His interest in Johnson was rivalled only by his interest in and love for his adopted city. He played his part in public life and was elected to (or perhaps "selected for" would be a more accurate description) the Corporation of Lichfield, a position which he retained, as Councillor and Alderman, until the day of his death.

In 1832 Mr. Lomax achieved the dignity of being elected Senior Bailiff, a position which corresponded to the present one of Mayor. During his year of office the city received a royal visitor — the youthful Princess Victoria, then heir to the throne and twelve years old. She was staying at Shugborough with her mother, guests of the Earl of Lichfield and had come to Lichfield to see the cathedral. Mr. Lomax had the honour of escorting her around.

Ten years later Victoria came to Lichfield again, this time as Queen Victoria and with her husband, Prince Albert. They were now staying at Drayton Manor as guests of Sir Robert Peel, and once again they were met at Lichfield by Mr. Lomax.

During the intervening years the Municipal Corporations Act had changed the face of local government and this time he greeted them not as Senior Bailiff but as Mayor of Lichfield.

The Lomax business flourished, and throughout his time in Lichfield its owner maintained a strong connection with the ecclesiastical authorities both diocesan and parochial. Many clergymen were among his customers and he acted as supplier, printer and publisher to the Diocese of Lichfield and the Dean and Chapter.

Lichfield in those days was a centre of the coaching business. Mr. Lomax's shop was only a stone's throw from three of the principal coaching inns, the Swan, the George and the Talbot. Travellers changing coaches with time to spare, or people visiting the city, would be drawn to his shop. Many of them would want to visit the cathedral, and would be looking for a guide book to direct them. No such book existed, so to supply the want Mr. Lomax, soon after his arrival in Lichfield, set to and wrote, printed and published his own. He called it, *A Short Account of Lichfield Cathedral, More Particularly of the Painted Glass . . . for The Information of Strangers. 1811. Price Two Shillings.*

The "Painted Glass" referred to was the 16th Century stained glass which had been brought to Lichfield by Sir Brooke Boothby from Herckenrode in Belgium and installed in the Lady Chapel. It attracted many visitors, as also did the "Sleeping Children" monument by Chantrey, erected a few years later in 1817.

In 1819 Mr. Lomax produced a second guide book, covering more ground than the first one. This was entitled, *A Short Account of the State of the City And Close of Lichfield* and as well as the cathedral described the city, street by street. It was illustrated by a number of rather crude woodcuts showing such subjects as the Sleeping Children monument, the old Lichfield Grammar School, the Crucifix Conduit and the old iron mace of the Guild of St. Mary's — a relic which at that time was in the possession of the Lomax family, but which later was restored to the Corporation of Lichfield.[2]

As well as his books, Mr. Lomax had also published woodcuts of the cathedral, suitable for framing and hanging. But as his business increased he looked about for something better and woodcuts were abandoned for engravings. These are a form of intaglio printing in which the engraver forms the image by engraving lines of varying depths with a sharp instrument on a copper plate. When the picture is complete these lines can be filled with ink which is transferred to the paper when it is pressed against the plate.

Engraving permits a much more delicate gradation of tone than a woodcut and also more accurate line. This is very noticeable when the pictures are photographed and enlarged as has been done for this book. Most of Lomax's prints carry two names — underneath, on the left the name of the artist who drew the picture, and on the right also underneath, the name of the engraver, e.g., "Shaw delin." and "Nevill sculpt." (Shaw drew and Nevill engraved).

The prints thus produced were used for several purposes. Some were printed on stiff card, for framing, and some were printed at the head of a double sheet of correspondence paper; what today would be called a "notelet". In fact it is possible in Lichfield today to buy notelets with Mr. Lomax's pictures on them; the wheel has come full circle.

For over seventy years these views were sold in the shop at the sign of the Johnson's Head, until the advent of photogravure and picture postcards made them redundant. They can still be found in collections and scrapbooks, and in recent years some of them, (suitably enlarged and framed) can be seen on the walls of pubs and restaurants.

The subjects that Mr. Lomax chose for his prints are of interest for two reasons. First, because they give some insight into his character, and second because they also show Lichfield changing in character during the first three-quarters of the 19th Century.

The series starts with two subjects dear to Mr. Lomax's heart — Lichfield Cathedral and Samuel Johnson. Fortunately they were also subjects of interest to tourists visiting Lichfield, as they still are. For this reason they were already being produced by London publishers such as Rock & Co. and Cadell & Edwards, and as we have seen, were being sold by Lomax.

When he starts to publish his own Lichfield scenes, it is interesting to note that they are nearly always of new developments — the coming of the railway, the new King Edward's School, the Corn Exchange, the new churches of St. Mary and Christ Church and the Public Library. In contrast there are few scenes of the older Lichfield. In spite of Mr. Lomax's long connection with the Corporation, neither the old nor the new Guildhall is shown. The mediaeval almshouses of St. John's Hospital and Milly's Hospital are absent and there is no sign of the Theatre Royal, built in 1790. However, we must remember that there is no definitive collection of Lomax prints; it is just possible that there were others which have disappeared over the years. If any reader knows of such prints, the author would be very glad to hear of them.

The subjects of this book are arranged in chronological order, according to the dates in the titles. These dates refer to the publication of the engraving which is not necessarily the same as the date of the original drawing. This often dates the engraving by some years.

A few of the prints are from my own collection, having been given to me by the late Alan Bull of Lomax's Successors, the last firm to own the business, but the majority of the subjects are from the following three sources.

Firstly, the William Salt Library, Stafford, the Librarian of which, Mr. Dudley Fowkes, I must thank for his help and for permission to photograph.

Secondly, the Johnson Birthplace Museum of Lichfield City Council to the Curator of which, Dr. Graham Nicholls, I likewise offers my thanks.

Lastly I must thank Mr. John Mott, solicitor. As present owner of the late Alan Bull's house he acquired not only the bust of Dr. Johnson but also many relics of the former Lomax's Successors which he has made available to me, for which I give due acknowledgement and thanks.

Lichfield
June 1990

Contents

THOMAS GEORGE LOMAX
photographed at Llandudno, 1861
aged 78

The Bishop's Fish Pool, Lichfield c.1800

LICHFIELD is built on the two sides of a shallow valley, into which flows two streams from the west — the Trunkfield Brook and the Leomansley Brook — and out of which the Curborough Brook runs to the east.

Over the centuries the inhabitants of the city have dammed the flow of water to form pools for various purposes such as fish pools, mill pools and in the 19th century to act as reservoirs for water supply.

At the beginning of the 19th century, when George Lomax came to Lichfield, there were three pools[3]. The most westerly of them, pictured here, was the Bishop's Fish Pool which occupied the space now taken up by the Museum Gardens. In mediaeval times it no doubt supplied the Friday lunches and dinners for the clergy living in the Close.

On the south side of the pool was an area of marsh known as the Swan Moggs from its proximity to the inn of that name. "Moggs" is a word peculiar to Lichfield, meaning a bog or marsh.

This print was published by J. Harwood of London and used by Lomax for a heading to notepaper.

10

London, J & E Harwood, 26 Fenchurch Street.

Nº 230. April 30, 1842.

Lichfield

Lichfield Cathedral and Minster Pool 1806

LIKE THE PREVIOUS VIEW, this is not one of Mr. Lomax's publications, dating as it does from four years before he set up in business in Lichfield. He must, however, have sold many of these in his shop for it was produced as a frontispiece to a history of Lichfield by Thomas Harwood, Headmaster of Lichfield Grammar School, published in 1806.

It shows Lichfield Cathedral from the south-west and the second of the three pools, the Minster Pool, which lies to the south of the cathedral.

Victorian engineers of the South Staffordshire Waterworks Company who surveyed the pool in 1856 gave their opinion that the pool had been formed by quarrying the sandstone which lies beneath. If so, this would have been for the Norman cathedral, built in 1088.

For centuries the Minster Pool acted as a mill pool for a water mill in Dam Street, while up to the time of the Civil War (1642–1646) it provided protection on the south side of the Close as a military fortification.

In the 18th century, at the suggestion of Anna Seward, the Lichfield writer and poet, Minster Pool was landscaped in imitation of the Serpentine in Hyde Park, London. Since then it has formed one of the many delightful features of the Lichfield landscape.

The print is taken from a drawing by T. G. Worthington, Esq., made in 1796, engraved and published by Cadell and Edwards of London in 1806. The scene is little different today.

C. Wild.... Pinxit.   Published by Messrs Cadell & Davies Strand Dec 3, 1815.   B. Howlett.

Stowe Pool, Lichfield c.1810

TO THE EAST of the cathedral lies Stowe Pool, the last of the trio. In 1810 it occupied a much smaller space than it does today and was much lower. It still worked a watermill by St. Chad's Church. This view of it by Charles Stanfield R.A. makes a fine scene with the stately pile of the cathedral as its centre. To its left beyond the trees can be seen the tower of St. Mary's Church; on the right rises Beacon Hill from where Sir William Brereton conducted the last siege of Lichfield Close in 1646, during the Civil War. Close by the cathedral is the white shape of "Hate House" or "Spite House" as it is called today.[4] On the far side of the pool is the group of houses known as "The Parchments" where Dr. Johnson's father had a parchment factory.

In the foreground the waggoners are manoeuvering the rear part of their timber waggon over the logs which will be slung from it before it is united with its front wheels. Nearby the fisherman is busy searching for something — perhaps the fresh water shrimps with which Stowe Pool is supposed to abound?

Lichfield Cathedral.

Lichfield Market Place c.1830

AGAIN, this is not a publication of Mr. Lomax's but one of which he must have sold many copies in his shop. It shows the centre of Lichfield as he must have known it when he came to the city, looking along Breadmarket Street from the west end of the Market Place.

St. Mary's Church, on the left of the picture, was the second building on the site, built in 1721 in the popular classical style of the period. It was the Guild Church which in mediaeval times had been the home of the Guild of St. Mary and St. John Baptist, the religious guild which was the predecessor of Lichfield Corporation. It was served by six priests who lived in Priests' Hall on the other side of Breadmarket Street.

At the far end of Breadmarket Street can be seen the Guildhall, from where the Guild, and later the Corporation, governed the city. Like St. Mary's it was the second building on the site, and in the same manner it was built in the classical tradition.

Nearest to us on the right hand side is the house and bookshop of Michael Johnson. Here, in 1709, was born his son, Samuel, later to achieve lasting fame as Lichfield's greatest son and one of England's foremost writers.

Although this print is not dated, the period can be identified fairly accurately. The third pillar of the house (the middle one) was inserted in 1826, and Mr. Evans, the ironmonger, whose sign is over the shop, left in 1830.

Dr. Johnson's Birthplace 1831

THIS WOULD APPEAR to be the first print published by Mr. Lomax himself. Not surprisingly he has chosen the subject from one of his chief interests — the life of Samuel Johnson.

Michael Johnson built this house in 1706 as a residence and for his bookselling business. For a struggling businessman who was never very well-off it is a surprisingly fine building and a good example of an 18th century town house.

Samuel Johnson was born and spent his youth here. After his death in 1784 the house was put up for sale by auction at the Swan Inn on the 30th July 1785. It was sold for £235 to another Lichfield bookseller, Major Morgan. By 1831, when this print was made it had been in succession a grocer's shop, an ironmonger's and now a newspaper office, the home of the *Lichfield Mercury*.

Already, by this time, it was being visited by those curious to see the birthplace of the great Dr. Johnson.

The engraver of this print was Nevill who did many later ones for Mr. Lomax. The artist's name is not given, but from the curious perspective of the Market Street side of the house it would appear to be by Caldwell, who later worked with Nevill and often got his perspectives wrong (Cf Trent Valley Station, p. 32).

This view was sold as a 7 inch x 9 inch print for framing.

S. Nevitt. Sc.

THE HOUSE IN WHICH D.ʳ JOHNSON WAS BORN.

Published & Sold by T. G. Lomax, Lichfield. 1831.

Lichfield from Pipe Hill 1840

WHEN MR. LOMAX said in his evidence before the Parliamentary Committee considering the Bill for the South Staffordshire Railway, "The conveyance of a small parcel to Walsall (by road) used to be charged eightpence, which is now one shilling and sixpence and great uncertainty in punctual carriage" he must have been thinking of the road in this picture, which shows the Walsall road at Pipe Hill, looking towards Lichfield.

This is the sight of the cathedral which still greets one today when descending Pipe Hill. Mr. Robson who drew this picture for Mr. Lomax must have stationed himself on the opposite side of the road to the Royal Oak, the ancient beerhouse built up against the sandstone rock at the side of the road halfway up Pipe Hill. No doubt he refreshed himself there when he had finished his work.

G.F. Robson delt.   Tombleson sc.

VIEW FROM THE WEST OF
THE CITY OF LICHFIELD.

Lichfield Published by T.G.Lomax 1838.

Drayton Manor, Staffordshire 1842

THIS VIEW of the home of Sir Robert Peel appears on notepaper stocked by Mr. Lomax in his shop, but was published by a London firm, J. Harwood of 25 Fenchurch Street. It is the only view known to the author which is not of Lichfield. Mr. Lomax probably included it in his stock in 1843 when Queen Victoria and Prince Albert stayed at Drayton Manor as the guests of Sir Robert Peel. It was on this occasion that Queen Victoria made her second visit to Lichfield where she was met by Mr. Lomax as Mayor of the City.[5]

Drayton Manor is now an amusement park, visited by thousands from all over the Midlands. Most of the buildings are gone, but the tower on the right of the picture still remains.

No author's or engraver's name is given.

22

London, J & F. Harwood. 26 Fenchurch Street.

Drayton House the Seat of Sir Rob.t Peel. Bart. M.P.
Staffordshire May 9, 1842.

St. Michael's Church 1845

S T. MICHAEL'S is one of the three mediaeval parish churches of Lichfield. It stands on Greenhill, in one of the largest churchyards in the country — seven acres in extent.

In 1842-44 it underwent a very thorough restoration, amounting almost to a rebuild and this print was probably commissioned to show it in its restored condition.

The architect responsible was Thomas Johnson, a Lichfield man with offices in St. John Street. Johnson was one of the first architects to become involved in the 19th century Gothic revival movement which was associated with the Oxford Movement and the Camden Society at Cambridge and which advocated the return to Early English Gothic as the true expression of Christian architecture in England. His restoration of St. Michael's was accordingly carried out on those lines. This picture is of interest as it shows the church as Thomas Johnson left it, later to be changed in 1890 by Oldrid Scott who favoured the perpendicular type of architecture.

Throughout all these changes St. Michael's has retained to this day the very fine royal coat of arms of Queen Ann over the chancel arch, the only church in this area to do so.

The artist of this drawing is not known, but could well be Thomas Johnson himself. No engraver's name is given.

St. Chad's Church, Lichfield (From the West) 1847

FOR CENTURIES St. Chad's has been a place of interest to visitors to Lichfield. Here Chad, the first Bishop of Lichfield, settled with his followers in 667 AD on what was an island in a watery valley. The church in this drawing is the 13th century church which still stands today. In 1847 it was still on an island, with Stowe Pool on one side and two little streams encircling it and joining on the far side. The house in the centre of the picture was Stowe Mill, occupied by Thomas Woodward, the death of whose thirteen year old son is recorded in St. Chad's register as being caused by "being caught up in the mill machinery".

Close by the church can be seen the roofs of Littleworth Cottages, built by the contractor who repaired St. Chad's after the Civil War, to house his workmen. Like so many "temporary" buildings they survived long beyond their expected life, in this case until 1950. To the right of the church a glimpse of Stowe House appears among the trees. With Stowe Hill, another mansion behind the church, these buildings comprised the hamlet of Stowe, within the boundaries of the City of Lichfield but quite separate from it. In 1847 it makes a delightful sylvan scene, but one which was not to last much longer.

S.CHAD'S. LICHFIELD. WEST.

Published by T.G.Lomax, 1838.

St. Chad's Church, Lichfield (From the East) 1847

THIS VIEW must have been taken from the front of Stowe House, for it looks straight down a typical 18th century "vista" of an avenue of trees with the spires of the cathedral in the distance. In the foreground one of the rushing streams that encircled the church can be seen. Away in the distance on the left the tower of St. Mary's Church, still in its classical form, appears.

During the Civil War St. Chad's was badly damaged by Parliamentary forces who occupied it. After the war the roof was raised by building a brick clerestory, and this can be clearly seen in this picture by the housing marks on the east wall.

The two pictures of St. Chad's are obviously a pair by the same artist but who this was is not known, though they are of a high standard. Nor is the name of the engraver given. In view of the scene being taken from Stowe House the artist may have been one of the Gresley family who were living there at the time.

Mr. Lomax published these in two sizes (each size from a separate plate of course), one being his standard "notelet" size and the other about four times as large for framing. Some of these are still to be found in houses in Lichfield and at sales.

S. CHAD'S. LICHFIELD. EAST.

Published by T.G.Lomax 1841.

Christ Church, Lichfield

CHRIST CHURCH is the youngest of the Lichfield parish churches. It was consecrated on the 26th of October 1846 and its parish was formed out of the parishes of St. Michael and St. Chad's. It came into being as a result of the generosity of Mrs. Ellen Hinckley and her desire to erect a memorial to the members of her families who had died before her. The full story is told overleaf.

When Mrs. Hinckley was building Christ Church she lived at Beacon Place, a mansion standing in its own estate near the cathedral. The estate comprised what is now Beacon Park and extended beyond the western by-pass. Christ Church was just inside the park gates, the house by the church being the Lodge.

For her architect Mrs. Hinckley employed Thomas Johnson, who had just finished work on St. Michael's. He produced a design in the early Decorated Gothic style, archaeologically correct as one would expect. The tower, for example, is designed to appear Early English below but Decorated above — the correct sequence of course.

The print shows the church as Johnson designed it; the present transepts were added later.

There is no record of the artist or engraver, nor is a date given. We know however that it must be after 1851, for the scene shows the large box tomb at the east end of the church which is that of Mrs. Hinckley's son, Hugh Dyke Ackland, who died in that year.

The Sleeping Children Monument
Lichfield Cathedral 1848

THIS not very flattering reproduction of Francis Chantrey's masterpiece, the monument to the Robinson children in the cathedral, was not published until thirty years after its subject was completed. The publication was probably prompted by the building of Christ Church and the consequent interest aroused in the story of its founder.

Ellen Jane Woodhouse was the daughter of the Dean of Lichfield and in 1801 she married the Reverend William Robinson, Prebendary of Lichfield Cathedral. He died of consumption in 1812, leaving his wife with two little girls.

The following year, while mother and daughters were staying at Bath, the elder of the two girls (also Ellen Jane) was preparing for bed and reached for something from the mantelpiece. There was a fire in the hearth; her nightdress caught alight and she died from the burns she received.

Before another year was out the stricken mother received yet another blow when the younger child, Marianne, died from consumption. In three years she had lost all of her family. In remembrance of them she commissioned Sir Francis Chantrey to make the Sleeping Children group for Lichfield Cathedral.

The work was shown at the Royal Academy Exhibition of 1817 where it created a sensation. The following year it was installed at Lichfield.[6]

Lichfield Trent Valley Station 1848

THE LAST COACH to run through Lichfield left the George Hotel on 11th April 1837. The railway had taken over, but came no nearer to Lichfield than Tamworth, Stafford or Birmingham. Mr. Lomax lost his many travelling customers and took up the cause of promoting railway travel for the city.

Ten years passed, however, before Lichfield achieved a place on the railway system as one of the stations on the Trent Valley line which ran from Rugby to Stafford. The line opened on 30th November 1847 and was operated by the London and North Western Railway.

The view is taken from the bridge carrying the Burton Road, looking north. The station house was in the Tudor Gothic style, very popular at that time, the architect being a man called Livock. Trent Valley Station moved to its present position, on the south side of the bridge, in 1871 but the old station remained in use as a dwelling house until electrification of the line in the 1970's when it was demolished.

The perspective of the picture is distinctly odd in places (the canopy pillars, for example) but the subject matter is of interest to students of railway history — note the early type of disc signal and the Robert Stephenson locomotive on the left.

At this time the Electric Telegraph Company was extending its lines all over the kingdom, and using the railways to carry their overhead wires. A telegraph station was established at Lichfield Trent Valley, and suddenly the city was in telegraph contact with every important place in the land.[7]

Caldwell. del.   Nevill. Sc.

TRENT VALLEY STATION LICHFIELD

St. John's Street Railway Bridge 1849

THE OPENING of the Trent Valley Railway through Lichfield was followed two years later by the arrival of another line, the South Staffordshire Railway. This ran from Bescot Junction on the other side of Walsall, through Walsall, Pelsall, Brownhills and Hammerwich to Lichfield and from there on to Alrewas and Wichnor where it joined the main line. When opened it gave Lichfield a service of through trains to Birmingham in one direction and to Burton-on-Trent in the other.

The shareholders and directors were mainly local people (Mr. Lomax had shares in it) and some care was taken to ensure that the railway did not intrude too much on the scene. So the bridge which carried the railway over St. John Street was built of stone (supplied by the Earl of Lichfield), decorated with battlements and heraldic devices and designed to look like a city gateway. It was, in fact, only a few yards away from the site of the old Culstubbe Gate.

The view shown is that of the south side of the bridge (St. John's Hospital with its row of chimneys can be seen through the arch). The large heraldic device in the centre has the leopards of England and the four smaller ones are those of Anson, Bagot, Forster and Dyott.[8] On the other side are similar shields showing the city arms of Lichfield and those of four bishops — Clinton, Hacket, Hayworth and Lonsdale.

There is some artistic licence in the scene, for it shows two trains passing in opposite directions, but the timetable never, in those days, made such a thing possible.

Once again, no artist or engraver is mentioned.

36

ST. JOHN'S BRIDGE, LICHFIELD.

City Station, Lichfield 1849

AFTER CROSSING St. John's Street the South Staffordshire Railway covered a distance of about two hundred yards before entering Lichfield City Station (more commonly known as "The South Staffordshire Station").

The station house was situated to the east of the present station, where the former goods shed (now a tyre depot) stands today. It was quite an imposing building in the Jacobean style, for it was the head office of the company containing the boardroom where the directors met. The picture well illustrates the situation of the railway line on the outskirts of the city with country stretching away on the right. St. Michael's Church is prominent on the skyline and just below it can be seen the iron bridge which is still there today.

In a very few years the area on the right was to become covered with industrial buildings (principally concerned with brewing) as the railway attracted industry to Lichfield.

The station itself is interesting for the complete lack of advertisements — the early Victorian railway builders had a great respect for the landscape through which they passed. Unfortunately this concern was not to last long. By 1884 when the present City Station was built things had changed.

The artist is Caldwell and the engraver Nevill, the same pair as for the picture of Trent Valley Station.

THE RAILWAY STATION LICHFIELD.

Published by J. G. Lomax 1849

The Corn Exchange, Lichfield 1849

THE REPEAL of the Corn Laws in 1846 removed the protection which British farmers had long enjoyed and opened the way for imports of grain from North America. To assist the home producers to meet this competition, many country towns built corn exchanges in which growers and merchants could meet.

Lichfield Corn Exchange was built by a joint stock company formed for the purpose. Its building coincided with a clearance of the Market Place, the whole development opening up the centre of Lichfield. Chancellor Law, who ten years before had placed his statue of Samuel Johnson at the west of the market square, had a vision of an open public space in the centre of the city, dominated by his statue. He persuaded the Corporation to demolish the Market Hall which occupied most of the square and himself bought some old houses at the east end of the square and demolished them, thus achieving his aim. The new Corn Exchange, close by the Market Place, incorporated a Market Hall in its ground floor which was then let to the Corporation. Above it was a dealing room, octagonally shaped with a rather fine lantern roof supported on hammer beams. Here the farmers and merchants were to deal around a ring. Next to it was an assembly hall for concerts and lectures.[9] Adjoining the exchange, at the Bore Street end, was the Bank House of the Lichfield Savings Bank. The whole complex was in red brick and stone designed in the Tudor style by Thomas Johnson, the well-known Lichfield architect, and his son. It opened in 1849.

THE EXCHANGE LICHFIELD.

Lichfield Cathedral c.1854

THIS IS ONE of several prints published by Mr. Lomax for framing and hanging, the size being 7 inches by 9 inches.

One would have expected such a print of the cathedral to have been published early on in his business career, but a glance to the right of the picture will detect the two distant spires of St. Mary's and St. Michael's. The spire of St. Mary's was not completed until 1854, so the print must date from that year at the earliest.

Gilbert Scott's restoration of the West Front, begun in 1875, has not yet started, so the date of the drawing must lie between those dates. However, from the clothes of the figures and other considerations, it is more likely to be near to the earlier year.

Many of these prints must have hung on Lichfield walls, and probably quite a few still do.

Nevill appears to have been the drawer and engraver of this work.

Stowe Pool from the Close 1855

WHEN GEORGE LOMAX came to Lichfield in 1809 this view of Stowe Valley from the east end of the Cathedral Close still contained all the features that had been familiar to Samuel Johnson and his friends — the ancient church of St. Chad at the far end of the pool, with the two eighteenth century mansions, Stowe House and Stowe Hill, behind it. By the church was Stowe Mill where the mill stream "carried the overflow of the lake down towards the meadows under a sloping, grassy, hillocky piece of ground, covered in springtime with primroses and violets nestling in mossy coves . . ." as a contemporary writer put it. On the north side of the pool was the famous "Johnson Willow" and close to it the remains of John Saville's botanical garden and Falconer's bath house where the 18th century gentry used to take the waters. True, the south side of the pool harboured some rather unpleasant tanyards, but they were far enough away not to intrude on this delightful scene of 18th century civility.

But in 1855 all this was about to change. Richard Chawner and John Robinson McLean had turned their attention from railways to waterworks and had formed the South Staffordshire Waterworks Company. (The first meeting of the Board took place in the City Railway Station). Their aim was to pump water from Lichfield through a pipe laid along the railway track to provide clean water for the Black Country. Stowe Pool was to be turned into a reservoir.

This scene shows the pool in its last year before the transformation.

Lichfield Museum and Free Library c.1860

IN 1856 MR. EWART M.P. introduced a bill into Parliament to promote public libraries. It was successful, and Ewart's Act provided financial grants to municipalities for this purpose. The first place to take advantage of the Act was Manchester; the second was Lichfield.

Although the Corporation of Lichfield were responsible for building the library, the prime mover in the project was once again Chancellor Law. He chaired the committee, laid the foundation stone on the 3rd of October 1857 to the accompaniment of a selection from Haydn's *Creation* played by the Band of the Staffordshire Militia, and afterwards provided at his own expense a fountain to embellish the building. At its official turning on, the band once again attended and obliged with Handel's *Water Music*.

The architects were Bidlake & Lovett of Wolverhampton and the builder was Lilley of the same town. Unfortunately Mr. Lilley did a piece of jerry-building which resulted in the north-east corner of the library resting on sandstone rock, while the south-west corner was built on eighteen feet of silt. It was not long before this corner began to sink, resulting in cracks in the building. The heavy buttresses which disfigure the structure date from this time, but the problem was not finally solved until the library was underpinned with steel girders in 1938.

In spite of all this it has survived to this day, the oldest municipal library in England.

Nevitt. Sculp.

Bidlake & Lovatt

MUSEUM & FREE LIBRARY,

PUBLISHED BY T.G. LOMAX LICHFIELD.

Dr. Johnson's Statue, Lichfield 1860

IN VIEW of G. T. Lomax's interest in Samuel Johnson one would have expected him to publish a print of his statue soon after its erection in 1838. If he did so, no copy of it has survived.

The statue was given to the city of Lichfield by James Thomas Law, Chancellor of the Diocese and Master of St. John's Hospital, a great benefactor to the city in many ways. By the time this print appeared, published by Rock & Co. of London, there were numerous photographs of the statue in existence, including several by the sculptor, Richard Cockle Lucas of Salisbury who came back in 1855 to touch up his work and had himself photographed doing it.

The print may well have been made from one such photograph with the figures added by the engraver, which would explain their ridiculous Lilliputian size (their heads should have come up to the tops of the railings). The standards at the corners are gas lamps, removed at the beginning of this century. The railings themselves went for scrap during the last war.

Market Square and St. Mary's Church 1860

THIS IS another Rock & Co. print bearing the same date as the one of the Johnson statue (25th October 1860). Again, it was probably engraved from a photograph.

The scene is of historic interest, for it shows St. Mary's Church in a state of transition. In 1852 A. G. Street designed the new Gothic tower and soaring spire which was completed in 1854. Lack of money, however, prevented the rest of the church being rebuilt until 1872 and so for eighteen years Lichfield had the curious sight of a classical church with a Gothic tower and spire.

At this time the Market Square extended right across to the shops on its north side, the whole area being cobbled, and Market Street ended at its junction with Breadmarket Street.

Rock & Co London No 3172.

Mr Moore's House & Monuments. 25 Oct 1860

St Marys Church, Johnson's House & Monuments, Leeds

Lichfield Grammar School c.1864

IN 1849 the old Tudor schoolroom was demolished and replaced by the fine new Victorian Tudor building shown here. The Headmaster's house next to it, with the top floor dormitories in which many of the former occupants had carved their names on the woodwork, remained. The name of the architect is not recorded, but after comparing the style of the building with that of the Corn Exchange (page 25), one would not be surprised if it were the work of Thomas Johnson and his son who incidentally had their offices just across the road. The artist is Shaw and the engraver Nevill.

There is no date to the print, and I have given it the year 1864 because of the shepherd with his dog and flock of sheep.

In 1864 Thomas Winterton, a farmer of Alrewas Hayes opened a market for livestock on a site beside the South Staffordshire Railway Station just around the corner from the Grammar School. It could well be that the flock of sheep are coming from an auction sale at Winterton's!

Lichfield Grammar School moved to a site at Borrowcop in 1903 and the buildings in St. John Street were sold. After some years as a private house they were bought by Lichfield Rural District Council for offices, the schoolroom becoming the Council Chamber. In 1974 they became the offices of the Lichfield District Council, which they remain to this day.

KING EDWARDS GRAMMAR SCHOOL LICHFIELD

Published by T. G. Lomax

Chancellor Law's Tomb 1864

THOMAS JAMES LAW, Chancellor of the Diocese of Lichfield and Master of St. John's Hospital was a contemporary of G. T. Lomax. He was a remarkable man, eccentric in many ways,[10] but a great benefactor of the city.

When St. Mary's Church received its new tower there was no public clock in the centre of Lichfield, at a time when every self-respecting town had one (the electric telegraph had made Greenwich Time available everywhere). So Chancellor Law offered a public clock in a tower to be built over his statue of Dr. Johnson. Reluctantly, the City Council turned it down, for which we must be grateful.

But Chancellor Law had the last word. When his wife died in 1864 he had a vault built for her in St. Michael's churchyard with a fine stone mausoleum on top, surmounted by a clock which was illuminated by gas! It is extremely unlikely that a faculty for such a project would be granted today, but this was no problem for Chancellor Law — he issued himself with a faculty!

In 1876 he joined his wife beneath the clock, which continued to tell the time to the people of Lichfield until well into this century, almost certainly unique in this country.

The print is by Rock & Co., embellished once again with those curious Lilliputian figures.

St. Mary's Church, Lichfield 1873

THIS PRINT, another by Rock & Co., was probably the last engraving to appear for sale at the Johnson's Head, for in the same year George Thomas Lomax died.

The picture is also a break with the past for it shows the church as recently completed in the neo—gothic style in which it remains today.

At this time St. Mary's was the principal parish church of Lichfield as well as being the Guild Church which every Mayor attended with due pomp and ceremony on the first Sunday after his inauguration. But as the twentieth century drew on and people ceased to live in the centre of Lichfield, congregations declined and the church fell on hard times. By 1975 it was in danger of being declared redundant. The community of Lichfield came to the rescue, however, and with the financial help of local authorities and Lichfield charities St. Mary's began a new life as Parish Church, Old People's Day Centre and Heritage Centre. Today it flourishes in this triple capacity.

Rock & Co. London, No 6655.

2 Dec. 1873.

St Mary's Church & Johnson's house & monument, Lichfield.

Epilogue

THOMAS GEORGE LOMAX died in the summer of 1873 and his passing was the occasion of much written appreciation of his professional qualities, not only in the local press, but also nationally in the world of bookselling where he was regarded as an authority on the works of Samuel Johnson.

The business was continued by his youngest son, Alfred Charles Lomax, described by the late Alan Bull as "A lover of Lichfield, its cathedral, its institutions, its traditions; a keen Johnsonian and a donor to whom the Johnson birthplace owes much. It will not appear singular that his calling of a bookseller should have surrounded itself with an almost Johnsonian halo.

"The traditions of an old-fashioned bookseller's profession, and the associations of the establishment were always in evidence . . . The atmosphere of Johnson had truly drifted to Lomax's and in his business the traditions of his father were scrupulously maintained . . ."

Times must change however, and one tradition which Alfred Lomax did not carry on was the publication of prints. Photography had taken over and soon picture postcards were to be produced to meet the demands of those requiring souvenirs.

Like his father, Alfred Lomax served Lichfield as a councillor and alderman of its corporation, being elected Mayor in 1885 and again in 1886.

In June 1901 Alfred Lomax retired from business and moved from over the shop in Bird Street, where his family had lived for eighty years, to 14 Bore Street. Here he died aged 83, in 1912.

On his retirement he had disposed of his business to Francis Henry Bull and Edward Wiseman who had both been employed by him. They continued to trade under the name of "Lomax's Successors", maintaining the old traditions of the firm, until it was sold to the Lichfield Mercury Ltd. in 1942. Finally, in 1969 the business closed after 159 years' service to the community of Lichfield.

The name of Lomax is still remembered by many Lichfieldians to this day.

Author's Notes

1. When Lomax Successors finally closed in 1969 Mr. Alan Bull, whose family had been in the business since early in the century, removed the bust and placed it in a position especially prepared for it in his garden. Through the courtesy of Mr. John Mott, who now owns the property, I was able to examine it. The bust is about fifteen inches high and bears the signature "Robert Perry, 1821".

   Unfortunately, at some time in the past the head has been damaged and the nose broken off (a small boy's stone perhaps?) so it is not possible to say if it is a good likeness.

2. The Iron Mace, now in the possession of Lichfield City Council, is reputed to be the mace carried before the Master of the Guild of St. Mary, the mediaeval forerunner of the Council. The first known mention of it is in the catalogue of Richard Greene's Lichfield Museum (1786) where it is described as above. From there is passed into the hands of G. T. Lomax when the museum was broken up and eventually was restored to the Corporation by the widow of Alfred Lomax in 1912. It can now be seen in the Treasury of the Heritage Exhibition at St. Mary's Centre.

3. There are now only two, the Bishop's Fish Pool having been filled in by South Staffordshire Waterworks in 1856 when Stowe and Minster Pools became part of a water supply scheme. The Bishop's Fish Pool became the

Museum Gardens, but reappeared in its former state for a few hours one Sunday in August 1987 when a torrential downpour of rain covered the sites of the former pools with floodwater.

4. The myth of "Spite House" or "Hate House" still persists in Lichfield. The story relates to the three daughters of Sir Thomas Aston, all friends of Samuel Johnson. Two of them married and made their homes in the two mansions of Stowe House and Stowe Hill, at the eastern end of Stowe Pool. From these two houses there is a very fine view of the cathedral seen beyond the pool.

The third daughter never married but lived alternately with her two sisters, until a family quarrel made her leave them. Out of spite she built the tall and rather ungainly looking house at the eastern end of the cathedral, thus spoiling the view for her two sisters.

So runs the story, but some years ago a thorough research by the late Mr. Frank Marston revealed that Spite House was built by the Revd. James Falconer and was never owned by the Aston family.

5. This was the second time Queen Victoria and Prince Albert had travelled by train. They drove from Windsor Castle to Watford where a special train was waiting for them with a royal carriage specially built by the London & Birmingham Railway. A four-wheeled vehicle, it was painted a dark claret on the outside and the interior

The Royal Railway Carriage and Engine

was upholstered in blue satin. The carriage was heated by steam generated by an oil burner under the floor. What appears in the illustration to be a circular mirror on the end wall of the carriage was in fact a bullseye lens through which an attendant on the other side of the partition shone an oil lamp when the train was passing through a tunnel.

As the Trent Valley line was not yet built, the royal train travelled via the London and Birmingham Railway as far as Hampton-in-Arden and then on to the Birmingham and Derby Railway to Tamworth.

The visit to Lichfield was made by road — Lichfield did not yet have a station. The royal entourage was escorted by a troop of cavalry — possibly of the Staffordshire Yeomanry — and entered the cathedral close under a triumphal arch of greenery surmounted with a crown.

Interior of the Royal Railway Carriage

6. Ellen Jane Robinson was married a second time to Hugh Dyke Acland of Killerton, Devon. By him she had a son, also Hugh, who died in 1851, and a daughter.

Mrs. Acland survived her second husband and in 1835 married a third time to Richard Hinckley, a Lichfield attorney. They lived at Beacon Place and, as already related, built Christ Church. Her daughter, Ellen Mary Woodhouse Acland, married a curate of Christ Church, the Revd. Frederick Vernon, in 1867.

7. In its early days the telegraph system was operated by a private company, not by the Post Office. The receipt shown here was issued in 1855 for a message sent from Birmingham to Lichfield.

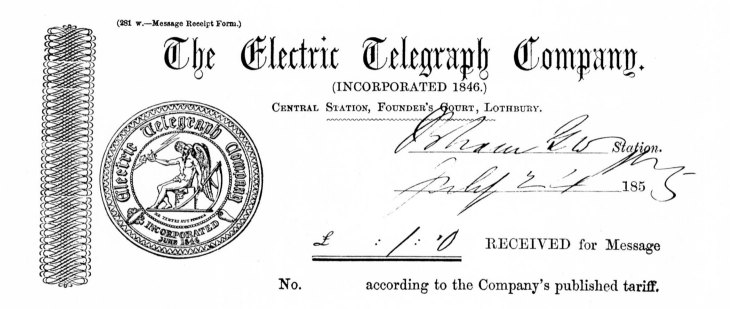

(281 w.—Message Receipt Form.)

The Electric Telegraph Company.

(INCORPORATED 1846.)

CENTRAL STATION, FOUNDER'S COURT, LOTHBURY.

_____ Station.

_____ 185

£   : / : 0   RECEIVED for Message

No.   according to the Company's published **tariff.**

8. Colonel Anson, Sir Charles Forster, Captain Richard Dyott and Lord Bagot of Blithfield were all directors of the South Staffordshire Railway Company.

9. Shortly after the Corn Exchange was opened a lecture was given in the assembly hall on the electric telegraph, at that time exciting great interest as a scientific advance in communication. For this occasion a temporary telegraph line was brought from the city railway station across Levett's Fields to the Corn Exchange and a telegraph station set up in the hall, messages being sent and received between Lichfield and Birmingham.

10. Chancellor Law was an eccentric in the great tradition of the 18th and early 19th century squires and parsons. Perhaps the best example of this is shown in the following notice, published by him and promulgated throughout Lichfield.

A FRIENDLY WARNING.

MR. CHANCELLOR LAW begs to give Notice to the HOUSE BREAKERS who got into his House on Monday Night, and passed within six inches of his bed's head, that he has sent away his Plate Chest; parted with his Silver Goods; and intends to use Plated Articles only for the future. MR. RYDER, the Head of the Police, has procured for MR. LAW a trusty Revolver; and MR. DENSTONE, who always sleeps in the House, is well armed. But MR. DENSTONE would be particularly sorry to send any of them out of the world in an act of sin, without time for repentance.

N.B. MR. LAW keeps his Money at his Banker's, and pays his Bills by Cheques.

LICHFIELD, October 31st, 1862.

Bibliography

The following works have been consulted in preparing this book:

Lomax, T. G.   *A Short Account of Lichfield Cathedral, More Particularly of the Painted Glass, for the Information of Strangers   Lomax   Lichfield 1811.*

Lomax, T. G.   *A Short Account of the State of the City and Close of Lichfield   Lomax   Lichfield 1819.*

Bull, Alan J.   *The Last Rush Job (The House of Lomax, 1810 to 1969)   Lomax Successors Lichfield 1969.*

Turner, Ursula   *Christ Church, Lichfield; A Brief History   Christ Church P.C.C. 1985.*

Marston, F.   *The 'Hate House', Lichfield, Staffordshire and Rev. Dr. James Falconer   Transactions South Staffordshire Archaeological and Historical Society 1970-71.*

Illustrated London News   December 1843.

Lichfield City Council Muniments.

Alfred Parker Papers 1925.